D0643760

VOLCANO

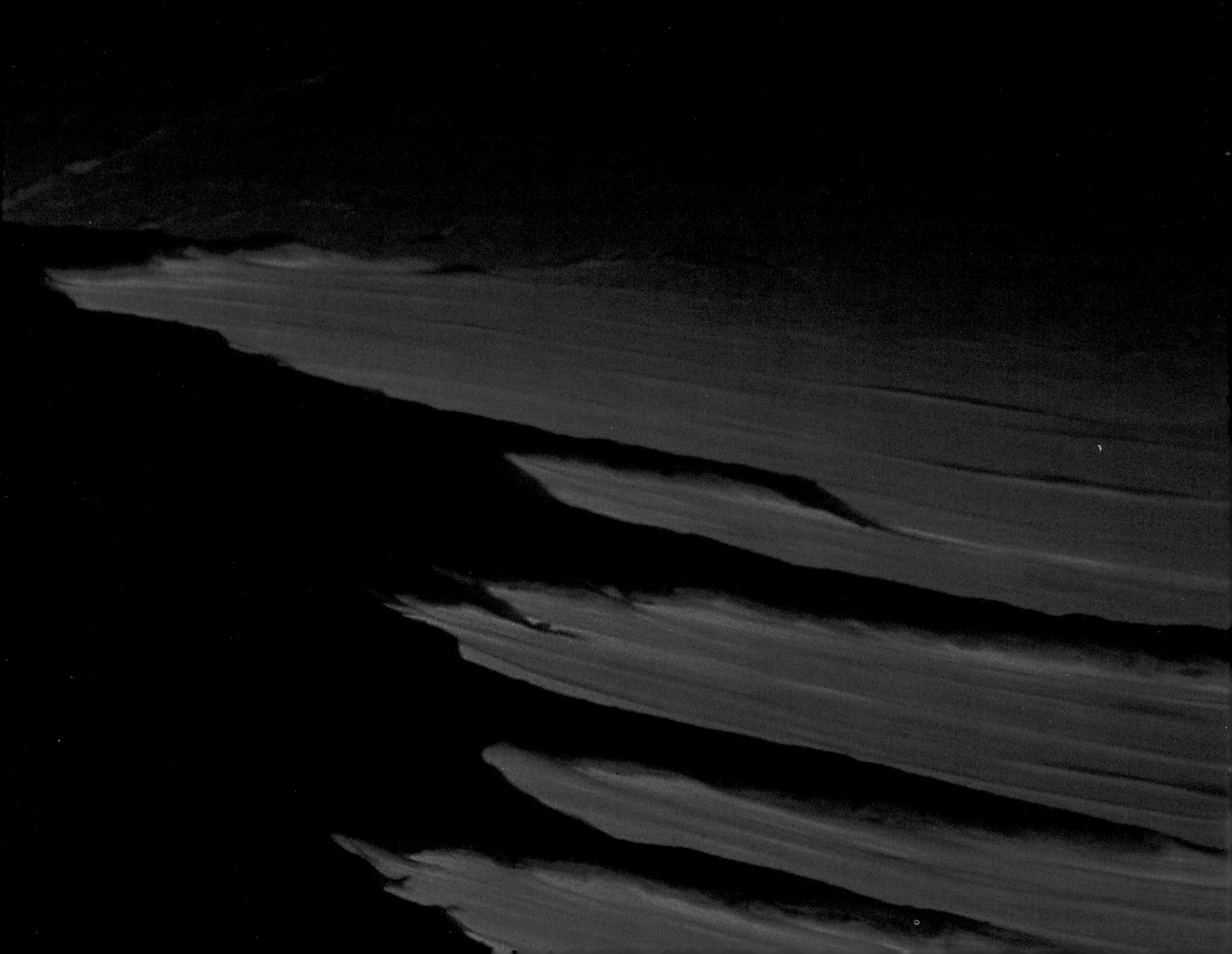

# VOLCANO

## CREATION IN MOTION

PHOTOGRAPHY BY G. BRAD LEWIS · TEXT BY JIM KAUAHIKAUA

MUTUAL PUBLISHING

ISBN 1-56647-672-0

Library of Congress Catalog Card Number: 2004111346

Design by Emily R. Lee

First Printing, October 2004
1 2 3 4 5 6 7 8 9

Mutual Publishing, LLC
1215 Center Street, Suite 210
Honolulu, Hawai'i 96816
Ph: 808-732-1709 / Fax: 808-734-4094
email: mutual@mutualpublishing.com
www.mutualpublishing.com

Printed in Taiwan

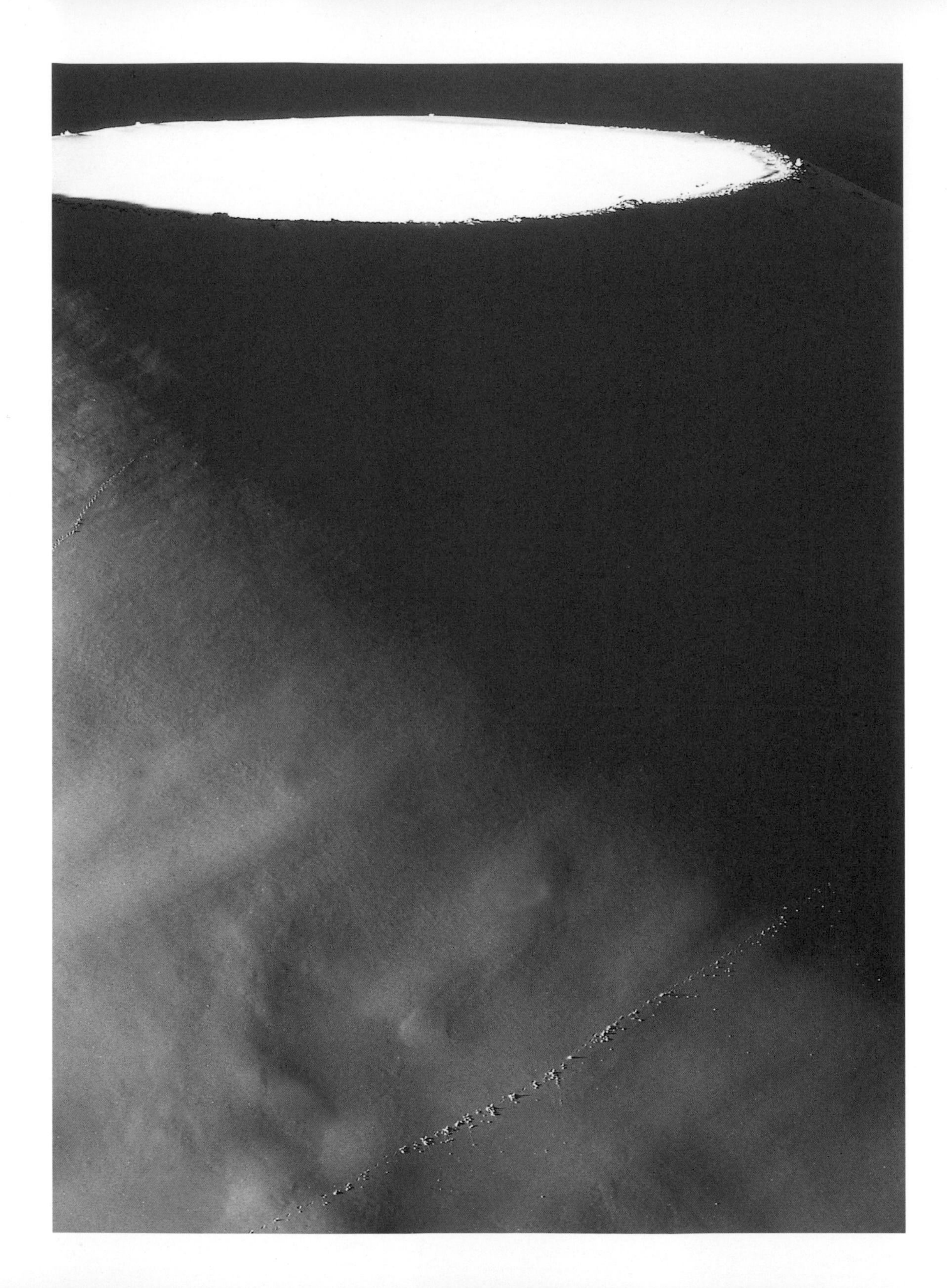

Brad Lewis talks about the volcano as if it is a relative. The volcano in question is officially known as Kīlauea, but commonly referred to as Pele, the fire goddess of Hawaiian mythology believed to reside at Kīlauea. Pele has personality and history. She has moods, and Brad has experienced many of them. He has lived on Pele's flanks for more than two decades and has seen the lava come down, destroying communities as well as creating new land. Brad has documented the longest continuous volcanic eruption of our time with commitment, sensitivity, and style. He is in the precious position to be a witness to a historic event that has significance far beyond the shores of the Big Island where it occurs. Some of us are fortunate enough to gain a few impressions of the raw power of this volcano. Pele, after all, does have a public face which has been seen by many during episodes when lava flows into the ocean. But Brad completes the portrayal of Pele's complex personality in a way that few people could. His coverage shows what commitment to place combined with artistry can do to bring a landscape alive for all of us, with respect and awe.

—Frans Lanting

# Dedication

This book is dedicated to Jim Kauahikaua,

whose continued presence on this planet is an

appreciated gift and a celebration of life.

# TABLE OF CONTENTS

from the staff at Hawai'i Volcanoes Observatory, Hawai'i Volcanoes National Park, and the Hawai'i Natural History Association. I would also like to thank David Okita of Volcano Helicopters.

The goal of my photography is to further the viewer's understanding and appreciation of the natural world and to contribute on a global scale photographs that help us comprehend the bigger picture. In this series of images, 'LavArt,' I utilize movement, light and texture of volcanic activity to open human emotions to the pulse of the Earth. I have chosen Kīlauea Volcano on the island of Hawai'i as my primary subject. Nowhere else on Earth is creation happening on a continual basis at such a rapid rate. I find it crucial that there exist visual reminders that the Earth is alive and fulfilling an agenda of its own. It is my desire to continue generating positive inspiration by focusing on photography that captures this essence of creation, beauty and raw power.

It has been a formidable challenge to capture striking images of this mountain of fire. The dangers are extreme at times. Thin-roofed lava tubes and spontaneous pit-craters are a threat. Where the lava flows into the ocean, large benches of land break away from the coast and fall into the ocean. I tread lightly and travel by intuition.

—G. Brad Lewis

# INTRODUCTION

he Hawaiian Islands are entirely the result of volcanic eruption. The hotogenic features of plants, birds, animals, and even humans and their omes, hotels, and resorts are mere adornments upon the island founation that was provided over many millennia by a string of volcanoes.

The process by which volcanoes build an island is full of drama and nysticism. Hawaiian volcanoes produce prodigious amounts of lava by arth's standards. And liquid lava is visually spectacular because it is subect and light source in one. Most things—a red t-shirt, or a green apple—et their color by reflecting a certain spectrum of light and absorbing the emainder. But at 2,100°F, lava is so hot that it emits red and orange light. hese explosions and molten rivers glow of their own accord.

The intense heat of lava is enough to cause forests to flash into fire nd ocean waters to flash into steam. The volcano and its lava release ulfur gasses adding an olfactory dimension. And the noise: sometimes t's so quiet you can hear the snap-crackle-pop of an advancing pāhoeoe flow, and at other times the gas jetting is so loud that you can't ven hear yourself thinking you should get farther away . . . quickly.

If you can't experience an active volcano in person, the next best hing is to see it through the eyes of a skillful and knowledgeable phoographer. You won't have the heat, the noise, and the smell of sulphur, ut you will see, with greater clarity and more permanence, incandesent molten rock transforming the landscape.

This collection of Hawaiian volcano images was selected from the ibrary of gifted artist Brad Lewis to introduce you to the diversity of orms Hawaiian eruptions can make.

# STILL IN PELE'S DOMAIN

## *Haleakalā • Hualālai • Mauna Kea • Mauna Loa*

Volcanic activity came to the Hawaiian Islands, Hawaiians say, because the volcano goddess Pele was just trying to get away from home—her parents, and especially from Namakaokaha'i, her jealous sister. Seeking her new home, Pele crossed the seas and first landed on an atoll northwest of Kaua'i. This place was far enough away from her family, but was otherwise unsuitable for Pele. She made her way down the chain, visiting each island in turn in search of the perfect place, to her current home at Kīlauea.

This epic story is sometimes given as evidence that Hawaiians knew that their islands get younger from northwest (Kaua'i) to southeast (the Island of Hawai'i, often called the Big Island). To a geologist, the story of Pele's search for a home shows that the Hawaiians knew even more than that. The story also explains—with surprising accuracy—how many of the volcanic features found in Hawai'i came to be.

The Pele story points out two things we now know. The Hawaiian Islands are volcanic and the noticeable differences in their appearance are due to differences in their age. Northwest of Kaua'i, only small, eroded volcano fragments and atolls remain. On the deep, rain-carved valleys of Kaua'i, the northwesternmost of the main islands of Hawai'i, volcanic activity ended five million years ago, while the volcanoes of the relatively smooth-flanked Island of Hawai'i are still very active.

The geological source of Hawaiian volcanoes is a hotspot, which has sent magma surging to the earth's surface for more than eighty million years. Magma punches through the sea floor and gradually builds a mountain of cooled, solidified lava. The hotspot, deep within the earth, is stationary—but the tectonic plates, huge shifting sections of the earth's crust, are not. Over the millennia, as the great slab called the Pacific Plate shifted slowly to the northwest over the hotspot at the rate of a few inches per year, the Hawaiian Islands were formed one after another.

Once magma bursts through the earth's crust, a volcano builds quickly. Some, like Mauna Kea, can reach heights of more than five miles above the ocean floor. As a volcano breaks above the ocean's surface, it loses its watery shield against the forces of erosion; wind, rain and surf start to carve the island. For a while, the sheer volume of flowing lava fills in the effects of erosion. But after a million years or so, volcanic activity wanes; the volcano is then at the mercy of the elements. Coral reefs grow around it. Massive landslides dramatically alter the volcano's profile, the broken rubble sliding far out onto the ocean floor. Wind, rain, and surf sculpt the new island into the valleys, bays and plains we know so well. Animals and plants make their way to the fertile soil that collects in the lower elevations. Humans may arrive and change the face of the island once again. Eventually, the island is worn away to sea level, and replaced by the coral reefs that once encircled it. Within ten million years of its birth, the once massive volcanic shield is reduced to a coral atoll, barely above the waves.

The story continues: when Pele sought her home, she brought along her digging stick, Pāoa. On each island, she used Pāoa to dig, trying to start a volcanic eruption. The stories say that these locations were generally at low elevations, and that the newly started volcanoes were quickly quenched by water, so Pele had to keep moving. The main islands already existed before Pele's arrival—she was looking for new eruptions. Again, the story describes geology: this is a remarkably accurate description of the brief rejuvenation of volcanic activity that every volcano mentioned in her story would have had, a few million years after vigorous eruption had ceased. Lē'ahi (Diamond Head), Pū o waina (Punchbowl crater), both on O'ahu, and Kalaupapa on Moloka'i are remnants of this late volcanic activity, and are just a few of the places Pele tested with Pāoa. These late-stage eruptions were probably brief, and featured much explosive interaction with seawater—just as the story says.

While the main Hawaiian Islands have been above water for several million years, Polynesians settled them only two thousand years ago. During this residency, Hawaiians have witnessed eruptions from five active volcanoes. From northwest to southeast, they are Haleakalā, on Maui; Hualālai, Mauna Loa, and Kīlauea on Hawai'i; and Lō'ihi, still beneath the ocean off the Island of Hawai'i.

Haleakalā, the only active volcano that has not erupted since Westerners came to Hawai'i in 1778, has erupted, on average, every few hundred years. Its crater was carved out by erosion well before Maui's main period of volcanic activity was finished, leaving multi hued sandy slopes and cinder cones within. When the volcano goddess Pele arrived on Maui, she was tempted to settle in Haleakalā Crater. This was the first location she had found that was safe from the quenching effects of water that drove her from the other islands, but Haleakalā proved to be too large for her to keep warm. She moved on to the Island of Hawai'i.

Mauna Kea and Hualālai on the Island of Hawai'i, like Haleakalā on Maui, are past the prime of their growth, and are starting to show the effects of erosion. Their summits also host smaller cinder cones that cover the smooth, shield volcano surface they sported in their youth. As with Haleakalā, their surfaces are weathering, and rust-colored hues are being added to the fresh blacks and silvers of cooled lava. Towering Mauna Kea even has a small, emerald-green lake named Waiau at its summit, perched atop layers of cinder and ash, over perpetually frozen ground.

Mauna Loa and Kīlauea are vigorous volcanoes still in the peak stage of growth. Mauna Loa, which last erupted in 1984, is said to be the most massive volcano on earth; it is so heavy that the Pacific Plate sags deeply under its weight. If the plate were more rigid, Mauna Loa might be more than two miles higher. The summit has recently shown signs of reawakening, but for now, all is calm. On the other hand, Kīlauea, Pele's current home, has been erupting steadily for the last two decades.

Lō'ihi Seamount, several miles offshore of Hawai'i Island, is still wholly underwater. It is a nascent volcano, just beginning its journey over the hot spot. Until recently, we knew Lō'ihi existed only by the earthquake swarms it generated. In the last few years, deep research dives have visited its summit, nearly a half-mile below the ocean surface, and have brought back images of the young volcano.

Pele's epic journey came to an end on the Island of Hawai'i. She thrives in a new dwelling place, the crater Halema'uma'u within Kīlauea caldera. Hawaiians consider the entire area sacred, and observe strict protocols of behavior there. Although the ways of the West dominate much of the island chain, at Halema'uma'u, Pele still rules supreme. And to Hawaiians, Pele is family.

# KĪLAUEA VOLCANO, PU'U 'Ō'Ō VENT

*The Cone • The Crater • Lava Lakes • Spatter Cone*

For more than two decades, the world's gaze has been trained on Kīlauea volcano. The current eruption started on January 3, 1983, when a long fissure opened in the forest and lava poured out almost ten miles east of the volcano's summit. Within a few months, the eruption had centralized to a single vent. All that lava pressed through one *puka* (Hawaiian for "hole") produced heart-stopping lava fountains. The next three years saw episodic fountaining until a second vent, Kūpaianaha, opened up in mid 1986, allowing a more constant outpouring of lava.

In four months, the more continuous flows from Kūpaianaha did what the episodic fountains from Pu'u 'Ō'ō could not—they reached the ocean. Pele has a hunger for fish, Hawaiians say, and when she desires, she can build tunnels, or lava tubes, to access the sea. During the sixty-six months that lava issued from Kūpaianaha, Pele must have had a strong seafood craving: she maintained direct access to the sea for forty-five months.

The change from fountaining to continuous flow also meant that Pele became more destructive. The lava fountains produced 'a'ā, flows that advanced quickly but were active for only a short time. The only homes destroyed were in a sparsely populated subdivision named Royal Gardens, directly downslope of the vents. Continuous effusion produces pāhoehoe flows. These move more slowly, but never really stop until the entire eruption is over.

It was during the time of Kūpaianaha that the lavas became most destructive. In March 1990, flows focused their devastating power on the coastal town of Kalapana. Ten months later, the town was no more. The flows moved in slowly; not a single life was lost. But more than one hundred homes, a store, and a church were lost to fire ignited by the constantly advancing flows. Several hundred people were displaced from their homes. In 1992, Kūpaianaha activity came to an end, and Pu'u 'Ō'ō once again became the center of attention. All the time that Kūpaianaha had been active, Pu'u 'Ō'ō crater had been widening, collapsing, and glowing, but not erupting. When activity returned to Pu'u 'Ō'ō, lava issued from its flanks and fed a lava pond within the crater.

Over the last several years, lava has erupted from the base of Pu'u 'Ō'ō and from vents within its crater. The flank vents have progressively buried the outer slopes, changing the silhouette of Pu'u 'Ō'ō time and again. Continued collapse has enlarged the crater to the size of fourteen football fields. The new, lower crater rim allowed lava to spill over the crater walls and run down its flanks. These overflows combined with the flows from the flank vents is creating a gently sloping, basaltic shield that is slowly engulfing Pu'u 'Ō'ō cone. If the current trend continues, Pu'u 'Ō'ō will soon be a massive, black, basaltic shield, with the remains of the original, tan tephra cone at its heart.

Activity inside Pu'u 'Ō'ō crater has changed over the years. Sometimes lava rushes out of one hole, flows across the crater, and drains into another hole. At other times, lava circulates inside a lava lake, and sometimes there is a large, solid island that appears to move slowly. For the last several years, several spatter cones have infrequently gushed lava. The constant flow has now filled the crater to the low points in its rim with solidified lava. And still, the eruption continues.

# LAVA FLOWS AND TUBES

## *'A'ā • Pāhoehoe • Skylights*

Any volcanic lava flow in the solar system is described in terms of two types of flow—'a'ā and pāhoehoe. These are Hawaiian words. Early western visitors picked the terms up from their Hawaiian hosts, and they are now used internationally to describe lava-flow terrain. The words describe very distinct flow forms that may differ in texture but not in composition.

'A'ā lava is covered with cooled lava fragments or rubble. Although the surface of the flow is partially solidified, the interior is still liquid. As the 'a'ā advances, the top of the flow moves forward faster than the liquid interior. Rubble falls off the advancing front, and is then overrun by the body of the flow, producing a motion not unlike the treads on an advancing bulldozer. 'A'ā looks clumsy, but it can move fast. During the 1950 eruption of Mauna Loa, the fastest-ever recorded lava flow ('a'ā) advanced at an average speed of just under ten miles per hour: a running pace. In the Hawaiian language, the word 'a'ā can also refer to burning, glowing, and fire—and to anger. Here is Pele in her fiercer incarnation.

Pāhoehoe lava, on the other hand, has a smooth skin, which can be very shiny when just formed. Pāhoehoe travels more slowly, and folds and ripples smoothly—the word pāhoehoe was later adopted by Hawaiians to describe satin. Pāhoehoe includes the word *hoe*, the Hawaiian word for paddle, which calls up the image of ripples in a glassy ocean produced with each stroke of a canoe paddler. Pāhoehoe shows Pele at her most seductive.

The goddess can change moods very quickly; a pāhoehoe flow commonly transforms into an 'a'ā flow as it traverses steeper slopes. Upon reaching relatively flat ground, an 'a'ā flow may stall and "bleed" pāhoehoe lava from its still liquid interior. If the 'a'ā flow is not advancing too rapidly, it may gradually change back into a pāhoehoe flow. Count yourself lucky if you witness these transformations.

Lava flows of any type require efficient, insulated supply systems to continue advancing. Lava channels, which carry 'a'ā, and lava tubes, which carry pāhoehoe, act as riverbeds and pipelines, respectively, through which insulated lava can travel fast and far. This intricate network of tubes and channels swiftly moves lava to the advancing flow fronts, often all the way to the sea.

Open channels allow bystanders to watch swift rivers of magma rush past, often flowing at thirty to forty miles per hour. Enclosed lava tubes, on the other hand, keep their secrets. Skylights, or collapses in the tube roof, afford the only views into active lava tubes.

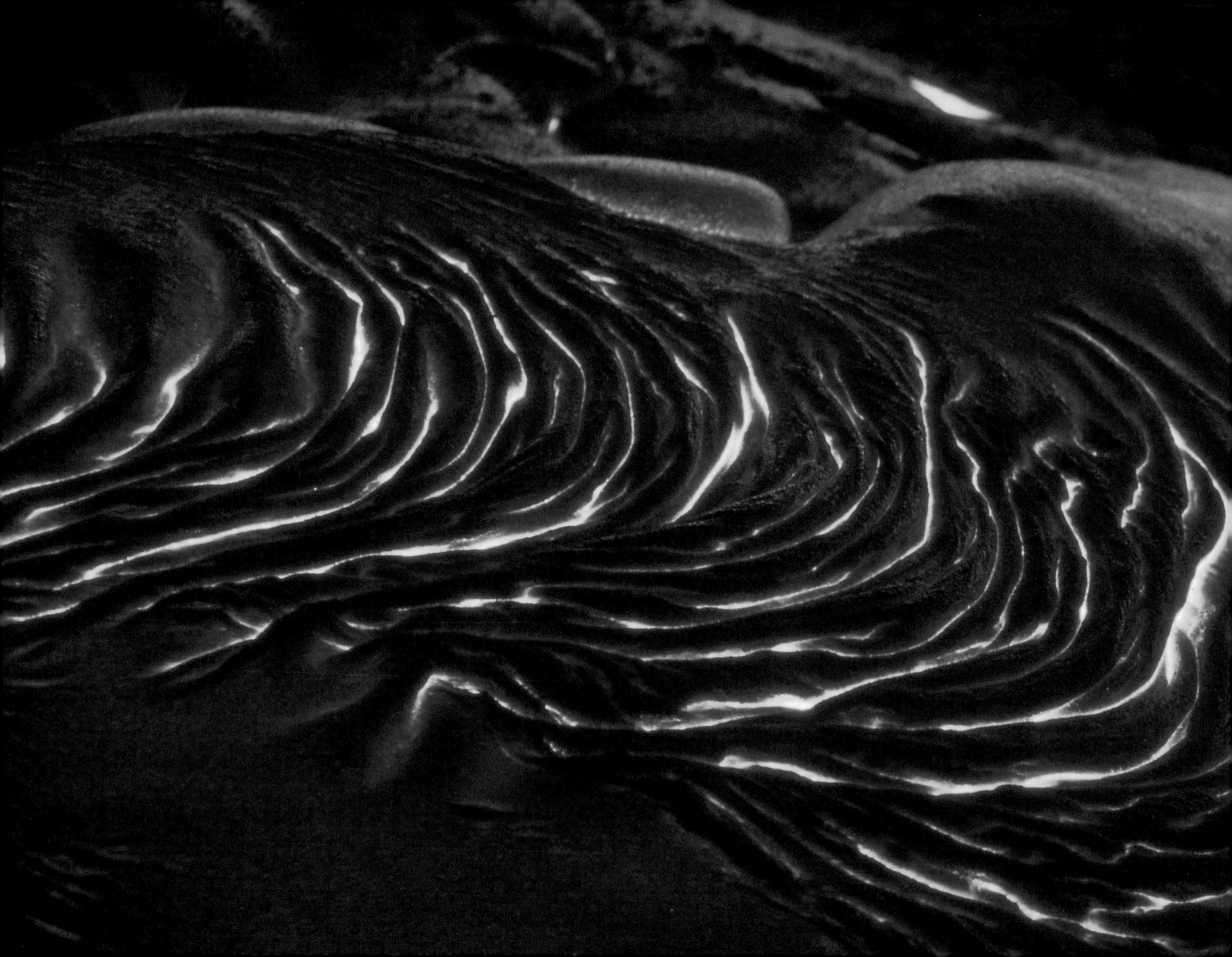

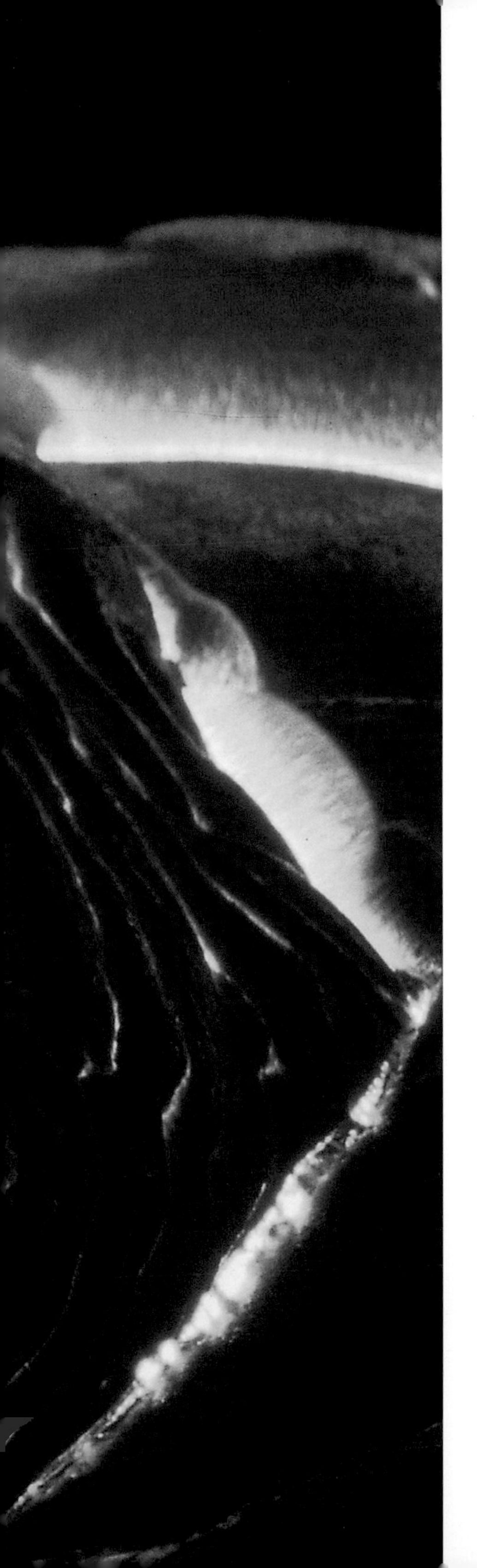

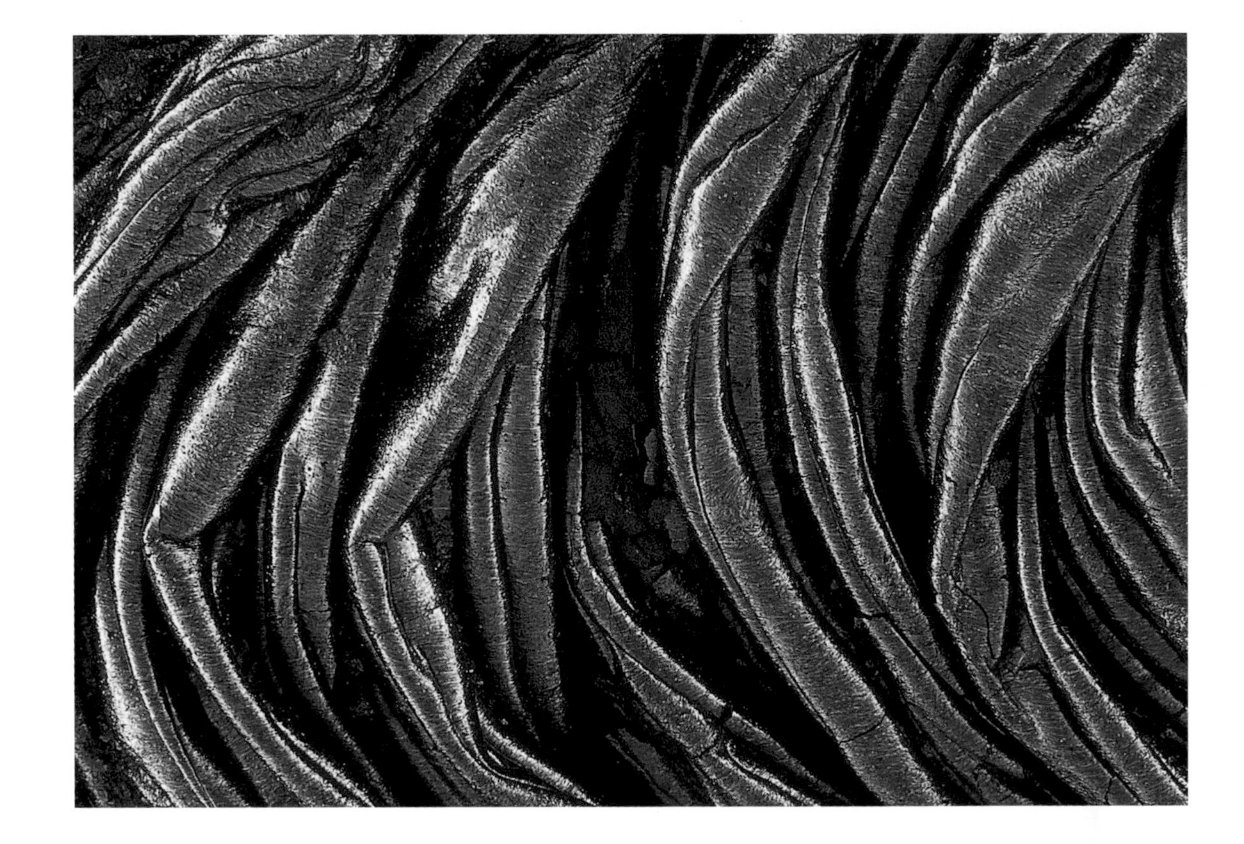

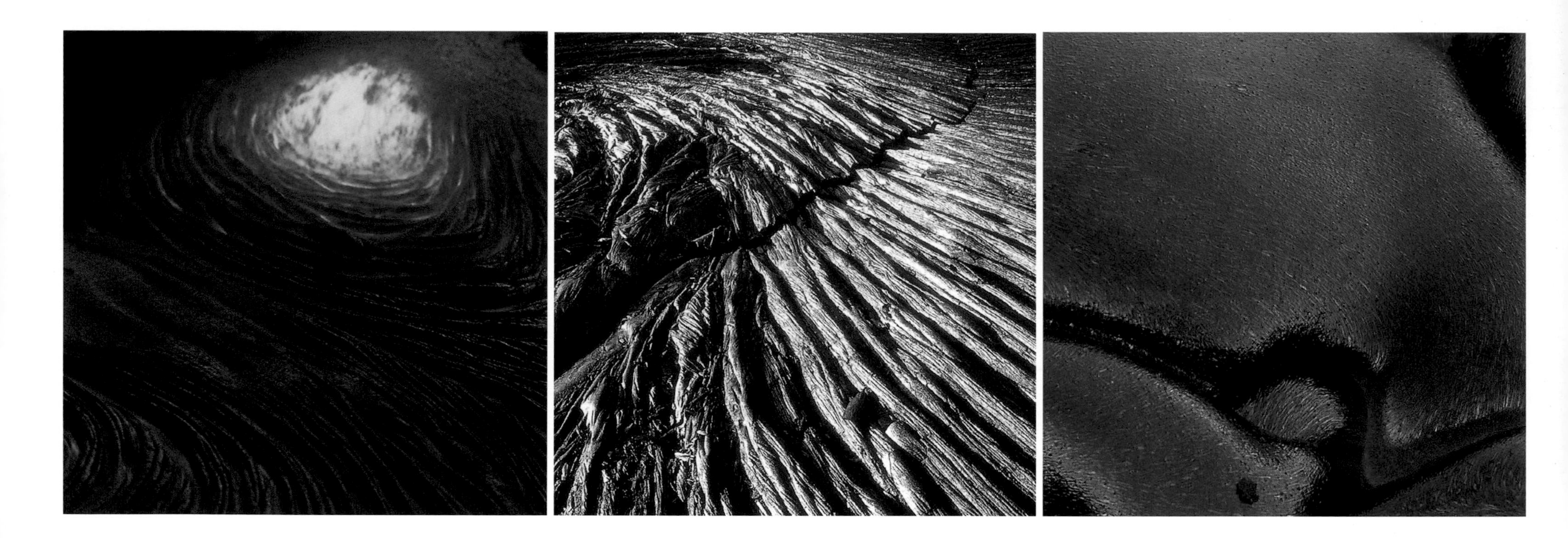

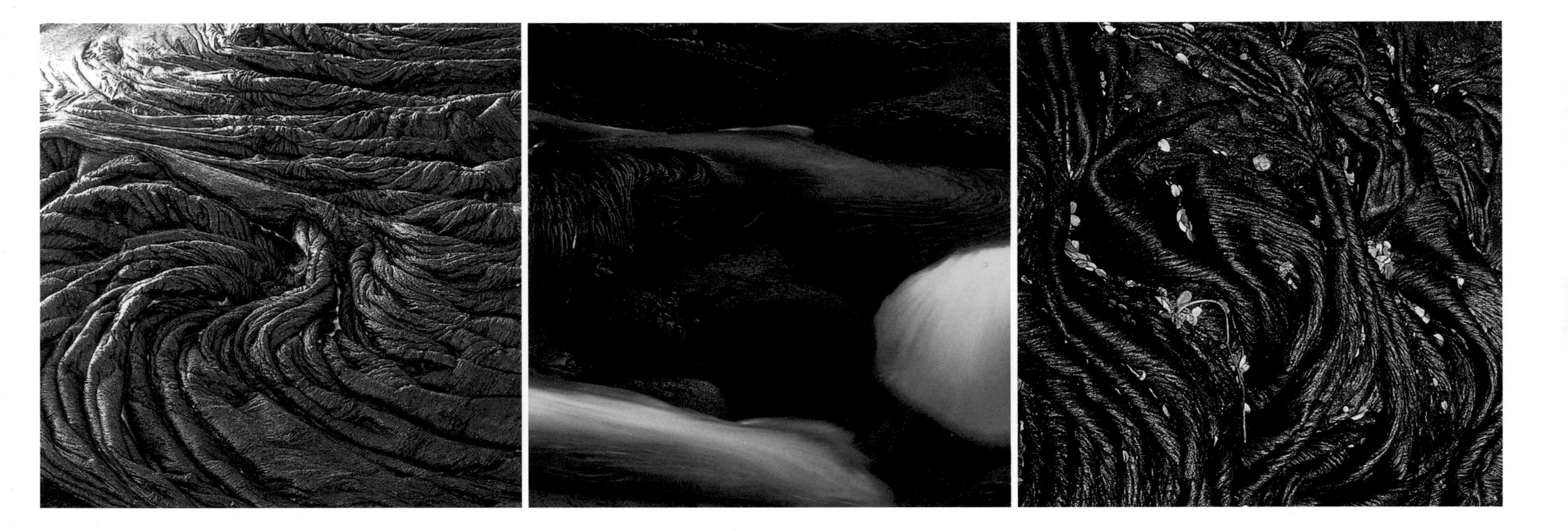

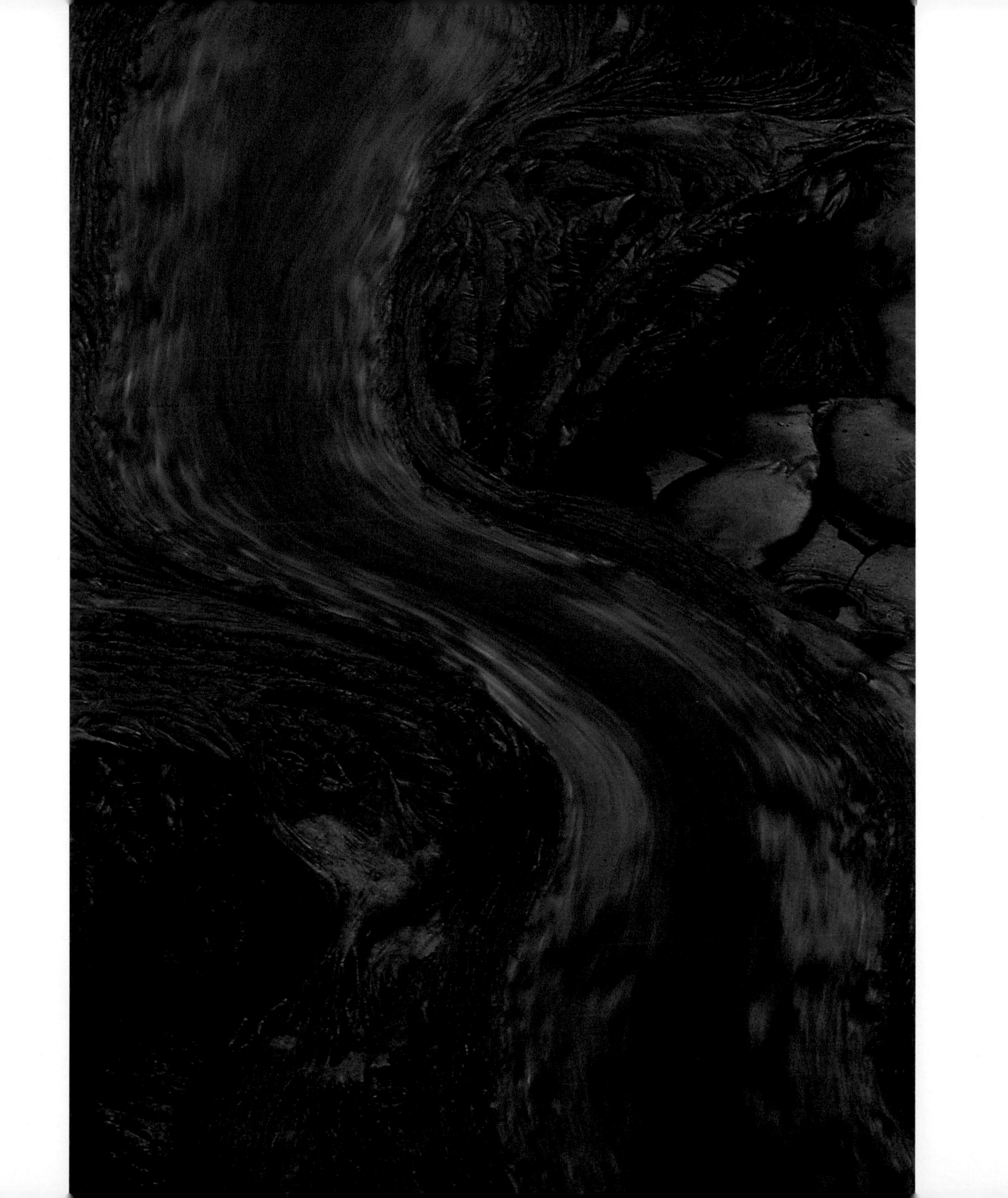

# FLOWS AND FOLKS

## *Kalapana • Visitors • Waha'ula*

Usually, the thing to do when you hear that a volcano is about to erupt is to get as far away from it as possible. Not in Hawai'i. People run towards Kīlauea when they get news of an eruption. This long-lived, relatively quiet and predictable eruption attracts lots of visitors, drawing both scientists and tourists. When the lava flows are within easy walking distance of a road, thousands visit the Hawai'i Volcanoes National Park each day. Abundant safety information ensures exciting and safe experiences by one and all.

Slow-moving lava and people can mix because people can move out of the way. Man-made structures are not so lucky. Lava flows have destroyed or engulfed many homes, a national park visitor center, a church, and a store, not to mention many miles of highway, and water and power lines. The town of Kalapana and the smaller community of Kapa'ahu were completely destroyed.

The most recent flows have mostly spared settlements, but have destroyed many acres of nearby native Hawaiian forest and parkland. Since 2002, the flows have been confined to the eastern edge of Hawai'i Volcanoes National Park, sparking a series of fires that burned through native forest.

STOP

LAVA FLOW
INFORMATION
AT VISITOR
CENTER
STOP
DO NOT
ENTER

WAHAULA VISITOR CENTER
NATIONAL PARK SERVICE
UNITED STATES DEPT. OF THE INTERIOR

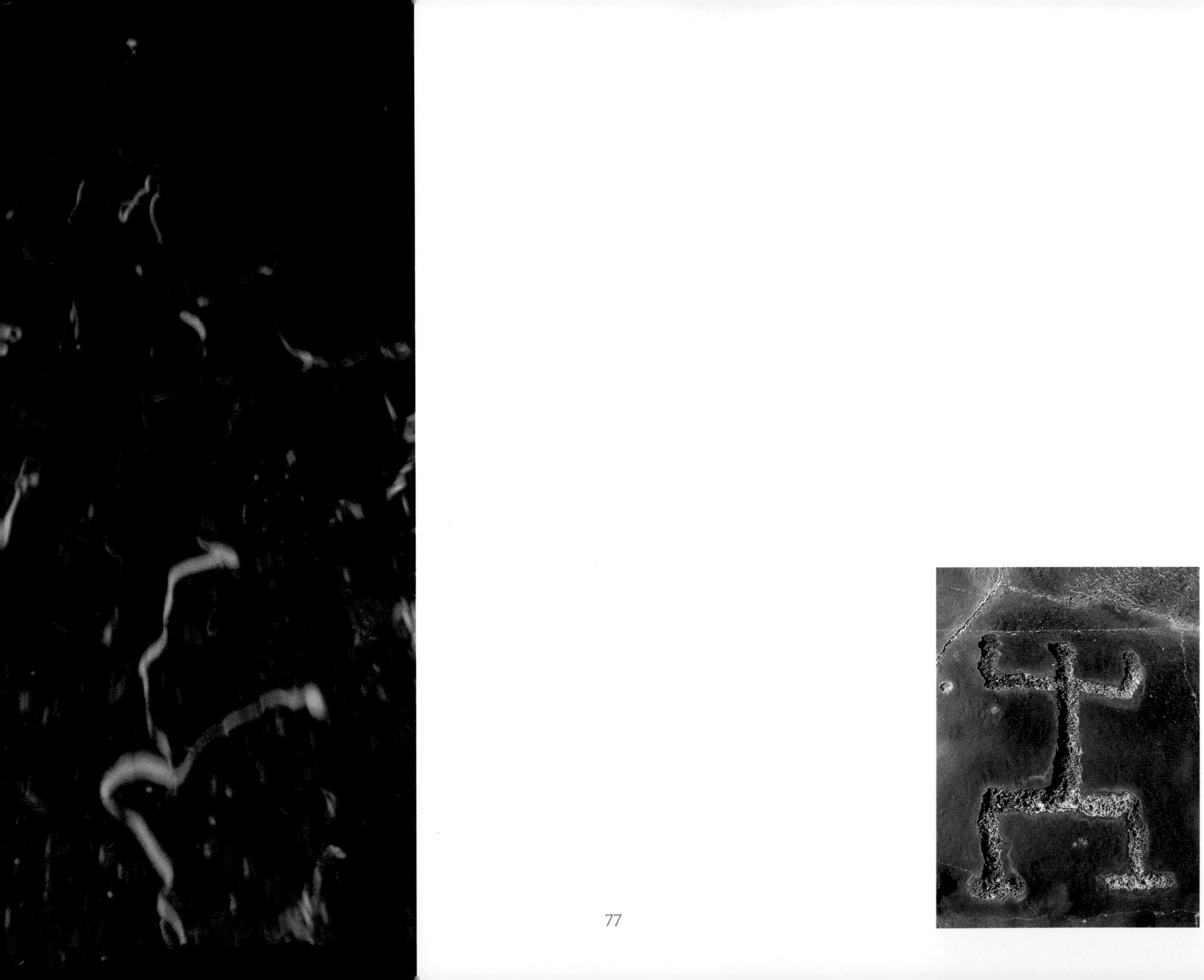

eight miles from the coast—a distance a determined lava flow can travel in just a few days. More often, though, the flow rushes downhill to the coastal plain, then dawdles on the flat ground for a week or more.

The first lava from a flow dips into the ocean cautiously, almost as if testing the waters, sending a slow finger of lava over a low coastal cliff. Flows drip over the sea cliff and collect at its base, while waves crash around the growing lava delta, sending up plumes of steam that are visible for miles. The drip becomes a channel, and can sometimes roof over, delivering increasing volumes of lava into the sea. As long as the lava keeps coming, the delta will advance into the ocean, creating new land while wave after wave eats away at its edges.

Each elemental encounter of water and molten rock takes a different form. Waves can splash hot seawater across even hotter lava, sending sizzling blobs of water skittering across the molten surface. Much of the water flashes into steam on contact. Sometimes, a small pocket of water trapped within molten lava will blow a large lava bubble as it expands rapidly into steam. Those molten bubbles explode, sending out a volley of flash-cooled fragments of volcanic glass that are carried high into the air with the acid-laden steam plume. Sometimes, a delta within Puʻu ʻŌʻō.

These points of entry to the sea are the most dangerous places for a bystander to be. The land may seem solid, but the new lava deltas and benches are fragile, supported only by unstable foundations of rubble and black sand. When conditions are right, the foundation will sag or shift and the deltas will crack, sending a section of bench crashing into the ocean. The movement of land will also disrupt the lava tube beneath, releasing the full force of the lava directly into the ocean, and causing an explosion of molten rock and seawater. Collapsing lava deltas have claimed most of the lives lost during this latest eruption. Yet these collapses are not without beauty. A severed tube can gush an incandescent fire hose of molten lava for many hours.

The sea is said to be the domain of Namakaokahaʻi, Pele's jealous and temperamental sister. When Pele and her sister meet, the manner of their greetings ranges from tender to tempestuous. The lava streams can be caressed by lapping waves as siblings can caress each other during affectionate moments. But the interaction can become instantly explosive like hot tempers between siblings who suddenly remember why they are angry at each other. Whichever it is, the meeting of these two powerful forces is always a sight to behold.

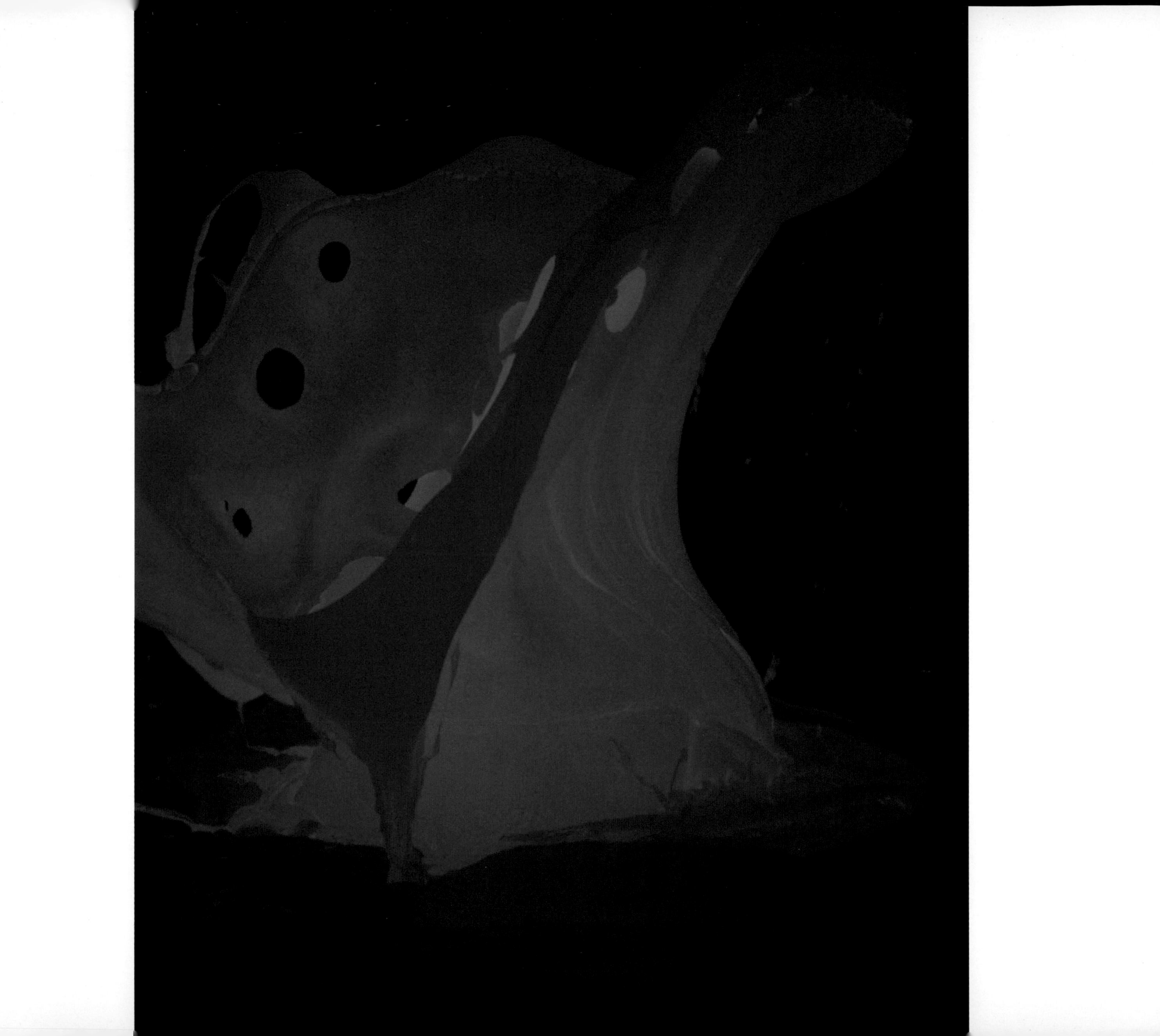

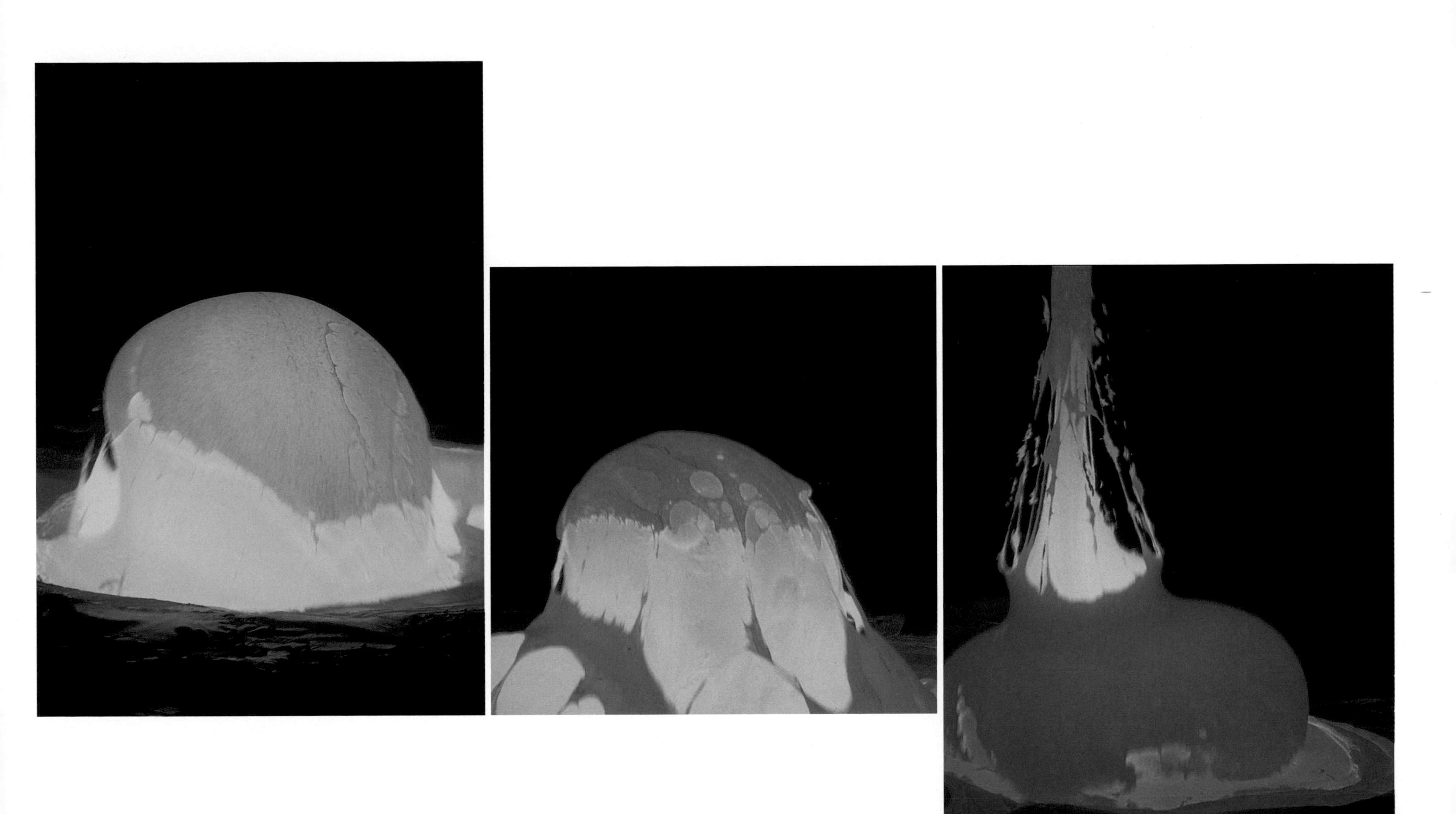

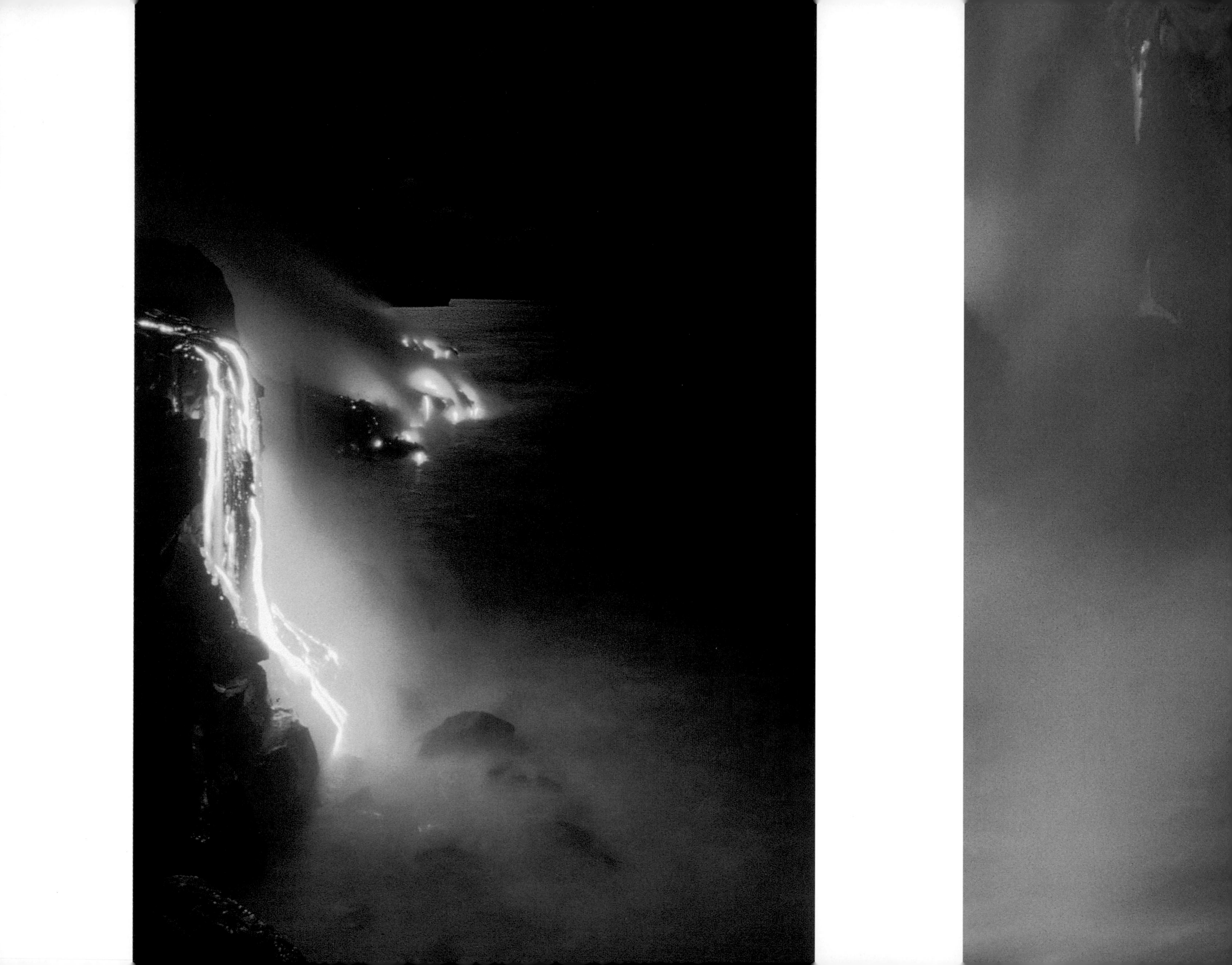

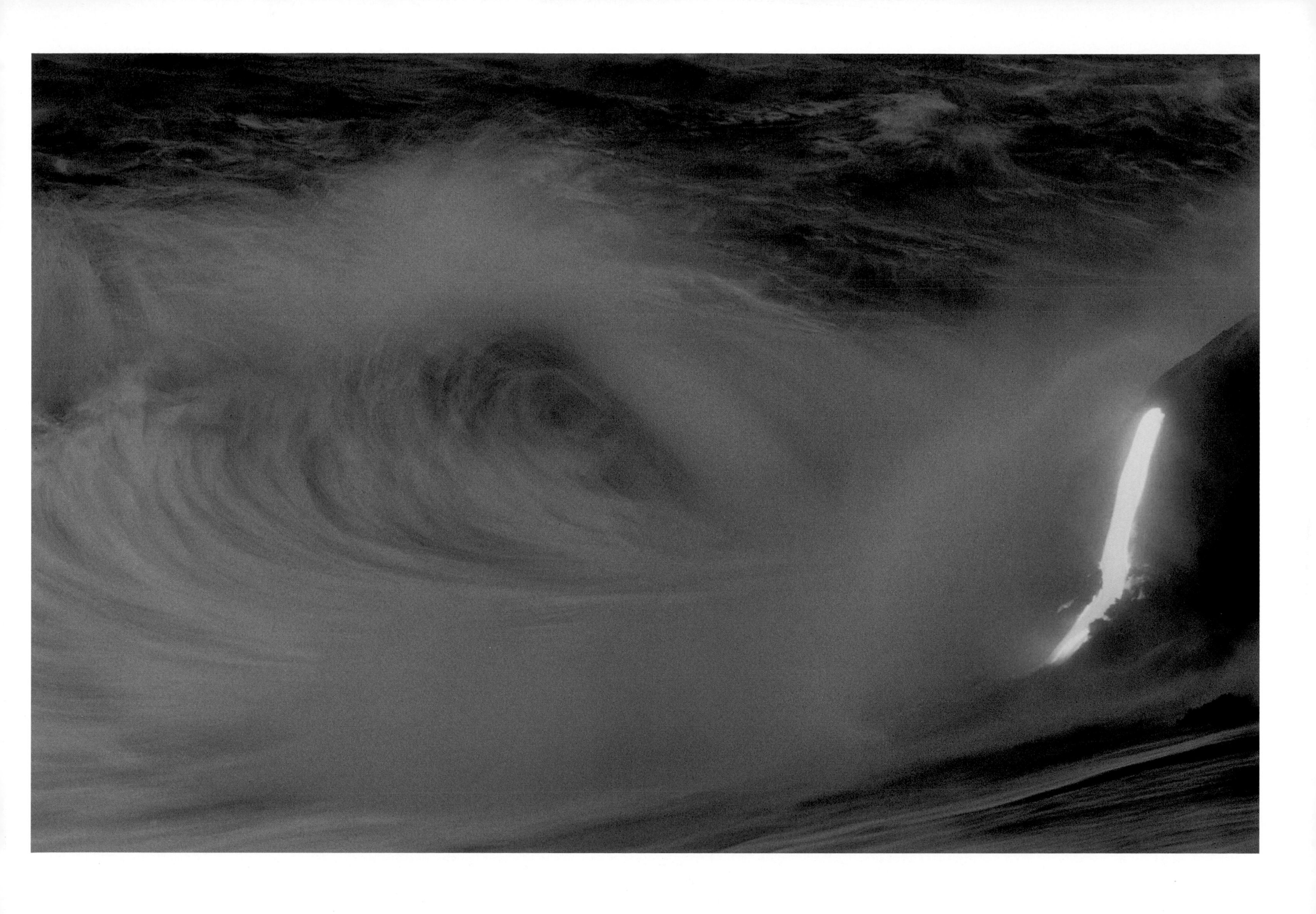

# VOLCANO CAPTIONS

**Page i** – Steam explosions throw lava bits into the air as lava pours into the Pacific Ocean.

**Page ii** – 'A'ā flow burning through low-land forest.

**Pages iv-v** – Fingers of hardened lava stretch downstream on the surface of this lava river.

**Page vi** – Snow-covered cinder cone near the summit of Mauna Kea.

**Page vii** – Ocean water enters a bench area through a breach in a lava tube, flashes into steam, blows, and bursts a huge lava bubble.

**Pages viii-ix** – Lava flowing out of a spatter cone on the south side of Pu'u 'Ō'ō rapidly fills the crater. The lava lake overflowed a few hours after this image was taken.

**Page x** – Aerial view of astronomical observatories on the summit of Mauna Kea, with snow-capped summit of Mauna Loa in the distance.

**Page xi** Lava pouring into the Pacific Ocean.

**Page xii** – Lava explodes high in the air in response to ocean water entering a lava tube. This dramatic action went on for many hours, resulting in a littoral cone.

**Page xiii** – Ribbons of lava from a bubble burst near an ocean entry twist into "limu o Pele." The cooled glass shards are paper-thin and have a greenish color, reminding Hawaiians of "limu," or seaweed.

**Page xiv** – Intricate folds, much like coils of rope, on the surface of cooled pāhoehoe lava.

**Page xv** – Bursting lava bubble.

**Page xvi** – The volcanic landscape of Haleakalā Crater on Maui includes erosional remnants of shield-building eruptions (foreground) as well as uneroded cinder cones (background).

**Page 3** – The remains of an eruptive vent, once covered by lava flows and now uncovered by erosion, Kalahaku pali in Haleakalā Crater, Maui.

**Page 4** – Early morning mist highlights ridges within Haleakalā Crater, Maui.

**Page 5** – Pu'u o Maui cinder cone within Haleakalā Crater, Maui.

**Page 6** – A series of cinder cones within Haleakalā crater.

**Page 7** – The summit of Hualālai backed by a shining ocean as seen from snowy slopes of Mauna Kea.

**Pages 8-9** – Snow boarder getting a thrill on the white slopes of Mauna Kea.

**Page 10** – Flank of snow-covered cinder cone near the summit of Mauna Kea.

**Page 11** – Twin ribbons of light made by car headlights at sunrise on their way to observatories near summit of Mauna Kea.

**Pages 12-13** – Sunrise snow slope of Mauna Kea.

**Page 14** – Various views of Mauna Kea. The middle image is Mauna Loa, with Mauna Kea in the background.

**Page 15** – Aerial view of Lake Waiau near the summit of Mauna Kea.

**Page 16** – Aerial image of the southwest rift zone of Mauna Loa.

**Page 17** – Moku'āweoweo, the summit caldera of Mauna Loa, with Mauna Kea just visible in the distance.

**Page 18** – Getting ready to move my tent for the second time in one night as a perch pond of lava overflows its banks sending a wide river of lava down slope. Active spatter cones are feeding a steady stream of lava in the foreground.

**Page 20** – Rivers of lava flow from a newly formed spatter cone outside of Pu'u 'Ō'ō.

**Page 21** – Momentary release of gas causes lava to spatter from the center of a lava lake inside Pu'u 'Ō'ō Crater.

**Page 22** – Dawn coming up behind Pu'u 'Ō'ō Crater of Kīlauea Volcano.

**Page 23** – Photographers record spattering cones of the East Pond Vent, within Pu'u 'Ō'ō Crater.

**Page 24** – Two spatter cones within Pu'u 'Ō'ō Crater at different times.

**Page 25** – Aerial view of Pu'u 'Ō'ō Crater with a circulating lava lake covering its floor.

**Page 26** – Nighttime view of a lava lake within Pu'u 'Ō'ō Crater.

**Page 27** – Nighttime view inside Pu'u 'Ō'ō Crater, lit by over a dozen incandescent cones.

**Page 28** – 'Ama'u fern growing from a fissure with Pu'u 'Ō'ō visible in the distance.

**Pages 28-29** – Time exposure of the Pu'u 'Ō'o lava lake full to the brim.

**Page 30** – Looking down on the surface of the Pu'u 'Ō'ō lava lake as old crust overturns and sinks while new crust forms.

**Page 31** – White trunks of dead 'ōhi'a trees stand within a kīpuka at the base of Pu'u 'Ō'ō.

**Page 32** – Active spatter cones inside of Pu'u 'Ō'ō vent.

**Page 33 - Left** – Large 'a'ā flow near the base of Pu'u 'Ō'ō Cone.

**Page 33 - Right** – Lava spit out of a cone within Pu'u 'Ō'ō Crater.

**Page 34** – Looking into the fiery maw of creation, Pu'u 'Ō'ō vent at night, with active spatter cones.

**Page 35** – Spatter cone on the outside of Pu'u 'Ō'ō vent, less than a day old.

**Pages 36-37** – Close-up of lava spatter being thrown into the air.

**Page 38** – Time exposure of lava spit out of a cone outside Pu'u 'Ō'ō.

**Page 39** – Spatter cone outside a gap in the west side of Pu'u 'Ō'ō Cone.

**Page 40** – A skylight reveals an incandescent wall inside a lava tube.

**Pages 42-43** – Still incandescent lava lobe folding its thin skin into pāhoehoe ropes.

**Page 44** – Cooled, ropy pāhoehoe lava.

**Pages 44-45** – The many skin textures displayed by pāhoehoe lava flows.

**Page 46** – A river of molten lava flows down a cliff face.

**Page 47** – 'A'ā lava flows over an old sea cliff, forming a new bench.

**Page 48** – Ropy folds of pāhoehoe lava.

**Page 49** – A fast moving 'a'ā flow courses down the pali, taking out all 'ōhi'a trees in its path.

**Pages 50-51** – A large 'a'ā flow inundates a lowland forest at the base of Pūlama Pali.

**Page 52** – Hot pāhoehoe lava toes at the base of Paliuli.

**Page 53** – Advancing lava burning sticks on a coastal flat.

**Pages 54-55** – A wide flow front sends many lava rivers over Paliuli.

**Page 56** – Jagged detail of 'a'ā lava showing the cooled cobbles on the outside and the molten lava on the inside.

**Page 57** – Fast-moving pāhoehoe river.

**Page 58** – Heather Lewis, my daughter, takes photos of a hot pāhoehoe lava flow.

**Page 59** – The remains of the Waha'ula Visitor Center burn after being torched by lava.

**Pages 60-61** – Lava flow coming down a driveway in Kalapana, shortly before destroying the house at the end of the driveway.

**Page 61** – Pāhoehoe lava toes about to cross the highway center line in Kalapana.

**Page 62** – Fire hydrant trapped in lava.

**Pages 62-63** – Lava flowing out of Kamoamoa campground exit, and crossing a road.

**Pages 64-65** – Lava flows sparked this fire which burned down the Waha'ula Visitor Center.

**Pages 66-67** – Lava flows burned many homes in Kalapana.

**Page 68** – Lava flowing into the ocean in Kalapana makes for some good fishing.

**Page 69** – Lava flowing onto the black sand beach in Kaimū Bay, Kalapana.

**Page 70** – Spectators watch lava flowing into the Pacific Ocean.

**Page 71** – Toes of hot lava flow into a water puddle on Kalapana road.

**Page 72** – This area at the base of Moa Heiau, Kamoamoa campground, glowed for many days before the lava even came close to it.

**Page 73** – Tree mold of burned out coconut tree, Kamoamoa campground.

**Page 74** – Spectators watch lava enter the Pacific Ocean.

**Page 75** – Photographer near the ocean watches huge lava bubble rise from the bench and collapse.

**Page 76** – A photographer records the dramatic action of lava bubbles exploding near the ocean at night.

**Page 77** – Ancient Hawaiian petroglyph carved in the wall of an old lava tube near Halapē, Hawai'i Volcanoes National Park.

**Page 78** – Lava flowing over a sea cliff into a rough ocean.

**Pages 80-81** – Lava flowing across a narrow beach into the Pacific Ocean at dusk.

**Pages 82-83** – Lava bubbles form intriguing shapes on a bench near the ocean.

**Page 84** – Lava flows into the Pacific Ocean as moonlight is reflected in the distance.

**Pages 84-85** – Streams of lava pouring into the ocean.

**Pages 86** – Sunrise image of a littoral cone that was formed during the night when ocean water entered a lava tube, throwing lava into the air.

**Page 87** – A pillar of lava is formed hours after first entering the ocean.

**Pages 88-89** – Lava flowing into the surf zone.

**Page 90** – Waves interact with lava flowing into the ocean.

**Page 91** – A vapor spout, on the right, is formed by the thermal disturbances in the air near a steam plume generated by an ocean entry to the left.

**Page 92** – A river of lava flows down onto a newly-formed bench at dawn.

**Page 93** – Incandescent lava bits mimic fireworks as they are thrown high into the air as lava enters the Pacific Ocean.

**Page 94** – Pāhoehoe toes moving across a beach beneath a lava arch.

**Page 95** – Time exposure of a lava river flowing over a sea cliff into the ocean.

**Page 96** – Pāhoehoe lava flowing around the base of a littoral cone at sunrise.

**Page 97 - Left** – Steaming hot rocks are washed up on the newly-formed black sand beach.

**Page 97 - Right** – Full moon above an ocean entry.

**Pages 98-99** – Rivers of lava enter the ocean.

**Page 100** – A river of lava flows over a precipice and into the ocean.

**Page 101** – Lava and moonlight illuminate a new point of land building out into the Pacific Ocean.

# About the Author

Jim Kauahikaua is the staff geophysicist at the U.S. Geological Survey's Hawaiian Volcano Observatory. Born and raised in Hawai'i, he has studied the formation and movement of lava flows and lava tubes for over a decade and has spent several memorable evenings with Brad watching lava. Jim currently lives in Hilo, Hawai'i with his wife, a cat, and two dogs on a very old part of Mauna Loa.

# Technical Notes

Volcano photography is hard on camera equipment, and I have gone through a lot of it over the years. Basically, anytime I am wearing a respirator to keep the caustic fumes out of my lungs, my camera is being slowly destroyed.

I often shoot with two camera systems at one time. 30 second exposures during "magic hour" is my favorite time to photograph the volcano, and I don't want to miss a moment during film changes.

For 35 mm, I use Nikon cameras with lenses ranging from 16 mm to 500 mm. In the medium format, I use the Pentax 67II, with lenses from 45 mm to 400 mm. Fujichrome is my film of choice. For digital capture, I utilize the Pentax *ist D. I use Gitzo tripods with the Arca Swiss ballheads.

—G. Brad Lewis

# About the Photographer

G. Brad Lewis is internationally recognized as a leading volcano and nature photographer. His volcano images have appeared on the covers of a number of magazines, including *Life*, *Natural History*, *Photographer's Forum*, and *Geo*, and within the pages of *Time*, *Outside*, *Fortune*, *Newsweek*, *Stern*, National Geographic, and many other publications. Additionally, Brad's lava and erupting volcano pictures have received numerous awards and been widely exhibited. Interviews with Brad have been broadcaste on the *NBC Today Show*, *CBS Evening News*, and the *Discovery Channel's*, "How'd They Do That?" Print interviews and photo essays of his volcano lava photographs have been featured in many magazines, including *Photo District News*, *DigitalFoto*, *Studio Photography & Design*, and *Outdoor Photographer*. His photographs are found in numerous private, corporate, and public collections around the world, as well as in fine galleries and through major stock agencies. Inspired by beauty and variety, Brad is based out of Hawai'i, Utah, and Alaska, traveling several months each year to pursue his art. He moved to the Big Island of Hawai'i in 1982, and lives there with his wife and daughter.